SONG OF LESS

JOAN FLEMING

Other publications by Joan Fleming

POETRY

Failed Love Poems
The Same As Yes
Some People's Favourites
Two Dreams In Which Things Are Taken

JOAN FLEMING

SONG OF LESS

First printed in 2022
by Cordite Publishing Inc.

PO Box 393
Carlton South 3053
Victoria, Australia
cordite.org.au | corditebooks.org.au

National Library of Australia
Cataloguing-in-Publication:

Fleming, Joan
Song of Less
978-0-6489176-3-2 paperback
I. Title.
A821.3

Poetry set in Spectral 10 / 14
Cover design by Zoë Sadokierski
Text design by Kent MacCarter and Zoë Sadokierski
Printed and bound by McPherson's Printing, Maryborough, Victoria.

 Cordite Publishing Inc. thanks Anwen Crawford, Joan Fleming, Penelope Goodes and Bella Li for their input during the production and editing of this book.

10 9 8 7 6 5 4 3 2

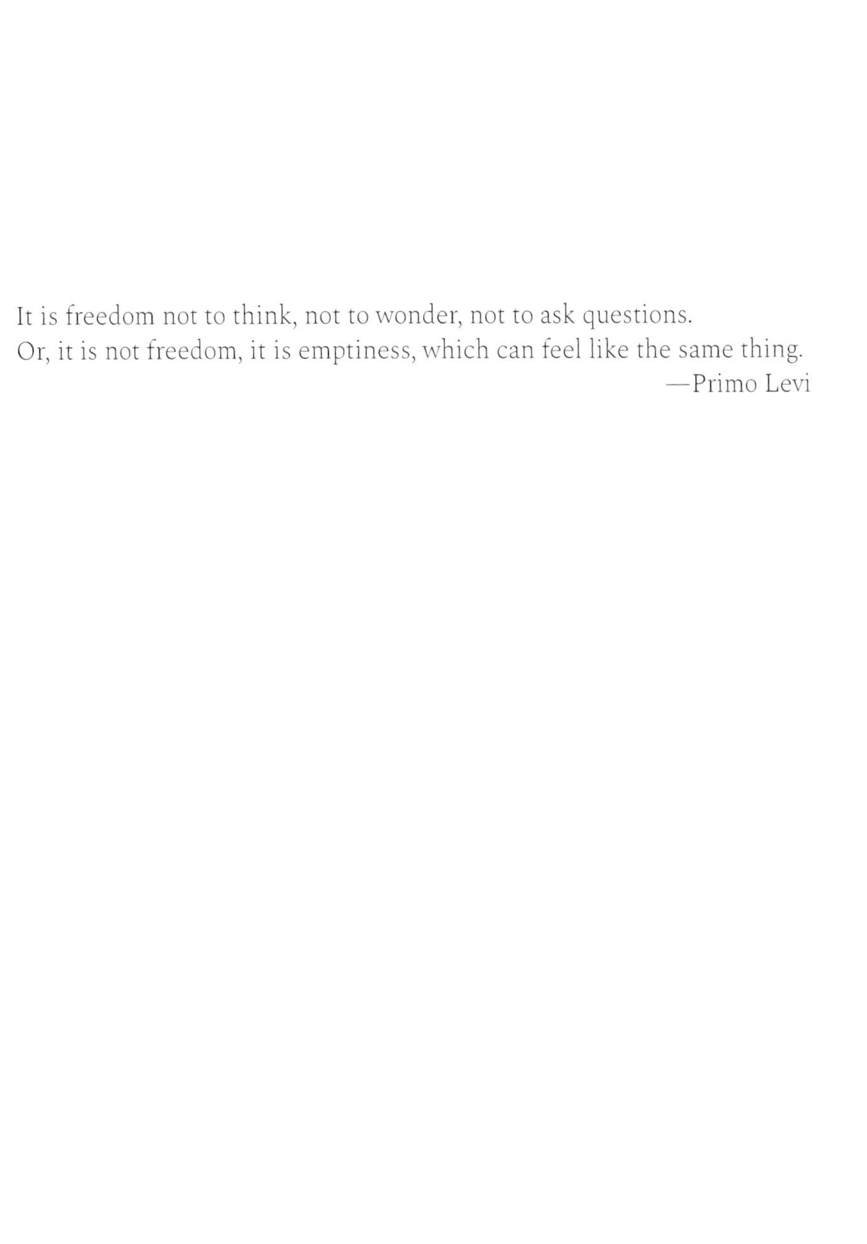

It is freedom not to think, not to wonder, not to ask questions.
Or, it is not freedom, it is emptiness, which can feel like the same thing.

—Primo Levi

CONTENTS

PREFACE

Madrid, Spain 2019 – the end of the UN Climate Conference – another moral failure on the part of those who could have made change. I go back to the labour union hall that all the activist groups have been using as a headquarters to help with the clean-up. There are only a few of us left. I take on the communal kitchen and bin heads of broccoli gone to dusty seed and half-used jars of slimy lima beans. I wash towers of greasy plastic cups with cold water and floor cleaner, because that's all there is. The door to the room that held the expensive sound equipment has been broken – no, not just broken, but thoroughly smashed. There is talk of a missing key, something lost in translation. The word 'smithereens' comes to mind.

In a back room littered with cardboard and paint tins, I find a giant papier-mâché head of a grandmother that First Nations activists fashioned for their part in the climate march. Alone in the echoing halls, it feels like silence and time are demanding something of me – an act of great care – though I don't know how to rise to it.

The crisis is upon us, but abstraction is a bulwark. Deafness, everywhere. We have come to an edge. I want to find a way of taking the truth into my body, and then putting it down into the ground. From somewhere offstage, a misery of voices begins to murmur in the scrounge. What starts up is a grief work. I wrap the grandmother head in a pall of plastic sheeting and carry it across the city to Librería Desperate Literature in the rain.

INTRODUCTION

A song exists because something has been added to the world. A voice strikes out, human or angel or bird. Hands clap together, skin against skin, or move upon an instrument made from a different animal. Catgut, turtle shell. Horsehair, ivory. Note for note a song carries through the air and our world becomes more because the song is on the air. Add electricity – the song now sounds across vaster distances.

Song of less, then: song of a world without the neigh of horses, cats or crooning dogs or magpies carolling. In this shadeless season, on this blistered earth, a small band of humans, some of whom receive the names of birds, in memoriam, are singing. They are trying to remember; they have tried to forget. They are making up something from the things that are left, which add up to more than nothing but are less than what has been. What might have been.

Once upon a time I heard a talk on climate change and grief; the presenter played recordings of insects in a certain forest, taped forty years ago, then taped more recently. The song of loss – the loss of songs – was palpable, but only due to the jumpcut in time between recordings. One would have had to listen so carefully to catch it as it happened, the singers extinguished in real time. This memory of change and loss, then, must be passed on. It is a part of what a song is for, and has been, in this land of so-called Australia, since time began.

The end already happened, the invasion, the apocalypse. Joan Fleming's epicedium is not taking place at The End; there will be no time like that. We will not get a time in which to sit and be enthralled by our own demise, like watching a movie. 'It is hard to believe I used to ridicule other citizens for their habits of entertainment,' recalls Yana, one of the company here, in a time that has arrived.

Our time of electricity. Our time of songs that have existed thanks to electricity, and how I loved those songs: the ones we wrote on plugged-in instruments and played on the radio and pressed onto plastic. Fossil music. And what did we know that we refused to know, when we sang those songs about the leaves being brown and the sky gone grey? Fossil prophecy.

Time will go on as it does, as we lose songs and their singers. In the absence of an End there will be no Beginning, no place from which we can make (up) the world again, out of whole cloth. We are left with what we are left with; we are salvaging.

The noun *salvage* dates from the seventeenth century: payment for saving a ship or its cargo from wreckage, or from piracy. The most valuable cargo in that century was human beings, captured and enslaved, the chief commodity of capitalism. We are still living in the wake of that history – everything, including this (end), has followed from it.

In *salvage* is a Proto-Indo-European root, *sol*: 'whole, well-kept', and this root, this ancient note, made its way into the word *holocaust*, in which the whole of things burn. *Holocene*: our epoch of many burnings. But also *solidarity*, this song we will keep singing in the wreckage.

—Anwen Crawford

YANA

In this new camp, I keep thinking – what can song do, anyway? On cave nights, I ask my love for a fresh tune, and he obliges, but then I come back to myself and the new songs I try to make are warped and wefted with the ones I have been carrying all along. What the child – oh lolly, freckled moonlight, *come let us adore him* – what the child managed with her drawings was to help us see the dilating Radius of what we had caused, and that glued us to one another as the feathers of a plucked bird are glued together by its blood.

I try, as Grandmother says, to hum it all facing backwards. But the mouth of me wants to tear up the hollow river right to the dust horizon, make the shattered dirt spit up its roots and sticks and fanbelts, take all that and make a tower – no – not a tower, there is another word, a thing birds make, a shape to show off.

What I long for is waste, extravagance, decoration.

Cousin Groundpigeon has found the uphill crouching way to prick a blister and spear the jellied heart in the single gesture that recovery requires. A starry heat spread into the cousins' faces as he lumbered into camp, carrying the globe of it in an unthinkable bare hand.

Cousin Frogmouth, who had acquired a chronic gash on his dragging foot, asked to be anointed and we watched as, open-mouthed, the borders of his wound fizzed and knitted over the days. When he no longer winced, he danced. A bird with a rubbery neck. A muddle of electrified cable.

How I missed the child then. She would be grown now, the age I was when we set out into the blistering green-desert with nothing in mind but continuation.

One night, a devil comes, loud on dusty wind. This is Groundpigeon's devil, the one with shreddings seething in his head where eyes should be. Blind, and infinitely reaching.

The devil reaches and reaches and reaches and suddenly I am on my feet beside Grandmother, a new sound spilling from my mouth, hot and spunk and pink as entrails. I hold the devil in my song as he goes through his changes, morphing into monster after monster, as he becomes every cousin.

Finally, he takes the form of my love, unscarred and wearing proper clothes. With a cry, I open up my arms and welcome him inside.

The blame he took on, as well as his love, is 'like a shadow on me all of the time.'

What does it mean to continue? Grandmother says that now is the time to ask ourselves what we are, other than ourselves. A piece. This is a moment mad for understanding. The body is a fence but it is also a wave and a thread in a fabric.

'All the leaves are brown, and the sky
                                                            is' a lid on this ruin of Story.

Lift it up.

(

the end

)

DON'T-BERRIES

The new immortals reigning in this dusk –
the plastics and the city's neon waste –
have given birth to legion berry us:
we trance the Endlings with before's sweet taste.

The tacky flyblown texture of their souls
nets every Endling's wish to keep their name.
The child whose line describes a thronging flight
alone can draw the quantum hum of Same.

Their fruitless scrape along the valley's throat
is companied by doppel-devil fear:
in seeping through the will-dies' paper skin,
we bring the peril of the mirror near.

We send their minds in backwards swarming call
to name, and own, the dark fact of the fall.

YANA

The moon organises time by yawning through our scrape-along and then yawning again. She glows like the screens we used to know and need. Along we sift til dust-thirty and dark in the hollow that used to be a river. Grandmother gathers up the don't-berries and thumbs them into the sack. At camp, it is loud with the hot winds. We pass the Ear around to hear the night's player. The green-desert woods are dressed in shredded packagings. Some of the surviving disguise themselves as Gone.

We are lucky Grandmother knows how to break up these roots for the white grubs they harbour. When we manage a fire, they taste like egg. Remember egg? In Reddy-by-the-Sea, I used to keep chickens. How annoyed I was when they escaped and tore up the garden. Now, we ourselves have all become something like a beak.

Yawning moon sings a song of less as we pitch our windbreak of scrap tin and seven gutted microwaves. We sleep in a row, with Grandmother on the outside because she knows the devils' names.

The job of someone every day is to carry the Instrument or to sit where the Instrument is while the rest go scrounging. The hills are dotted with the red blisters we must avoid, and the lilac spears of the trees the heat stripped quiet while we told ourselves a different story. The Forgetting comes in heaves like the racing drills of the dust twisters. Tonight, it is my turn to play the Instrument. I'm charged with 'California Dreaming', 'Total Eclipse of the Heart', and a hymn that gets louder before it ends.

Asleep, we don't scrounge, but sometimes our dreams do.

Grandmother is praying in circles

Safe back east

Safe to the water She has forgotten that no one is going anywhere like that again. Some days, the dim sky is scored by whitish trails, but we are not thinking of rescue. I was there when the Radius bloomed over the cities. There is nowhere to be rescued to.

I haven't talked about the other cousins. Bad days, they tangle.
You wouldn't want to see their faces.

The cousins help Grandmother slow-burn the don't-berries to make a druggy ash. Every yawning moon we mix it with the altered tobacco and rock and hum in a circle, and we visit our caves. Grandmother sings us through. My heart cave is a velvet painting of stars in which I hang suspended, with precious rocks embedded in my skin. It's here I get to see his face again, the rust and pepper of his beard, his split-shine eyes. He touches my body like he used to. It hurts and I need it. The don't-berry nights are exhausting. Grandmother says they are necessary. The next day, it is always difficult to walk into the hot winds and not keep our eyes shut against them.

It could be the thick, grey-green water from the compromised well that causes the forgetting. It is our only source. I no longer recognise my hands as those I used to have, back in the Reddy. The muscle all down my right-hand back is hard as a boulder from digging in the scrounge. Yesterday, I thought I saw a cat but it was one of the cousins pulling his bad foot behind him.

One night, a devil comes. It has pairs of ears all over its head. Grandmother stands up from where we are sleeping in our line and yells its name. She yells and yells. Rage is viscous. It has a human name. It cannot hear her. All its ears are stoppered with a brassy glinting stuff that sparkles when the devil, advancing, drops to all fours and whips its head like a dog with a sneeze coming. The distance of pale dirt between the devil and the rag pile of the camp beds closes and closes. An asymptote. We all are shaking, unable to look away. Grandmother loses her voice.

Yesterday, I thought I saw a bird

but there are all kinds of quick shadows now.

We have lost Cousin Shrike to the red blistering. We wrap him and place him in the Trees. Grandmother is teaching me to weave the new bedding. If you tear the gone cousin's blanket into strips it releases the imprint of his songs, which must go with him. We weave the strips with a weft of plastics and when I start to get the hang of the tension, the result is almost pleasing.

New gusts today leave nothing where we left it and the camp is quilted with worry. Grandmother is in Forgetting again and the moon is desperately tired. I speak with Cousin Groundpigeon: has he mastered the unblistering? Land is rashed, the cousins have their sharpened wood and they want to use it. The blisters, we think, harbour a cure inside their red sick bubbles. Technique is crucial, but the Almanac is in Forgetting too and can't open without Grandmother. Steady Grou is restless with his lance as we talk through the risk. He leaves the dirt pocked, ready for a spatter of seeds we don't have, and couldn't water.

I remember the city as a place of comfort specificities packaged in neat pottles of plastic and glass. A place of eyes shining with wine and meat, a place of sirens and lettering, machines of dispensation and waste tucked out of sight. The screech and heat of the metro – all that jostle I could never spare heart to look in the eye. It is hard to believe I used to ridicule other citizens for their habits of entertainment. Those sensations are gone to me now. Instead, I remember the feel of closing a window. I remember the taps. How they ran.

A long, low sounding tips from Grandmother as she comes back to – she whistles for Whiskey and Mum before the last of the Forgetting dissipates. We all miss the dogs.

Grandmother spits dirt, smoke, rind, and heaves herself up clapping. The cousins unfurl themselves from the Trees where they had slept half-wrapped in limbo, dreaming of hamburger and milk and compact discs.

The beak of ourselves is never not hungry. Against the song's advice two cousins have copulated and a seed is stuck in the womb's tubing and the one cousin is going painwards. We keep watch, shuddering the Instrument even though it is 'day'. Onceupon, we could make new people – city days with backyards and a rubbish of feathers. Cousin Twig, clutching at her centre, begs us never to stop at all.

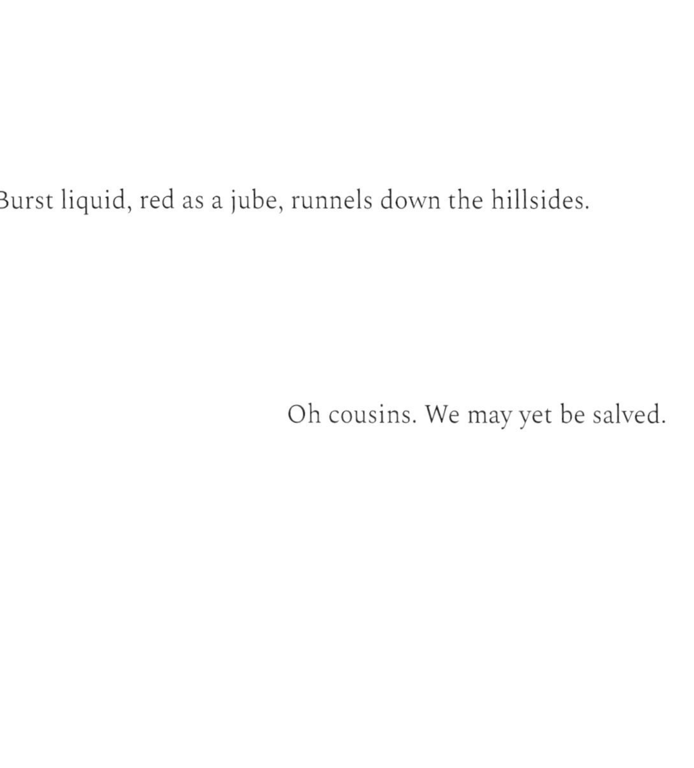

Burst liquid, red as a jube, runnels down the hillsides.

Oh cousins. We may yet be salved.

Yesterday, I thought I saw him moving towards me, stone blue eyed in a dust twister. I fell to my knees, letting the mean firewood I'd scrounged up scatter. You're out from the cave, I said but my mouth was garbled with want and dust, my tongue unpickable as a knotted plastic shoe. I closed my eyes to feel his hand approach me. May this blistered world be nothing to do with him. I closed them and closed them –

COUSIN TWIG

When the pain started up I thought
it's hunger again it's hunger
I didn't know nothing
I used to call something else hunger in the Reddy
but it wasn't
it was never
this

They carried me from the river hollow, dry and white and gritting
where I had been doing my shoulds
I'm a cousin you know
so
I scrounge

I used to be
not this
used to be a bow and a button
used to have long hair and every day I'd pull it
through a hot iron make it lustrous
used to have high shoes
and a face

When the pain hit it was like a cave visit only upside down with fire
I lost my left-side vision for a time
As we well know my right-side vision got clenched and lost
in the drizzle and stayed that way, so
I'm familiar

But I was thinking oh my fucking almanac there hasn't been drizzle
for this entire green-desert time
and what in the fire is happening

they tell me I was calling out for ice cream
well, Grandmother says pain makes confusions of us all

I remember before I lost my wakeness
I was thinking of what I recall from the Reddy
like
sweets are a sometimes food and never
hand a pair of scissors over blade first and never look at
the full cup of heat you're carrying in your hand
and it won't spill

like
all my little pocks and kinks I could fix right up
if I had the right pottle
as we well used to know
like
how much is enough? as some old king said
just a little bit more

In this new world it is never full dark
and never full light
but we always know when it is morning
How, I don't know
don't ask me

The cousins often say to me
hey, Twig
might you stop your crying now
I have been something of a weeper
as we well know

Then one day in the scrounge with a wet and weeping eye
Cousin Groundpigeon came up and put his hand on me
like nothing
like a cousin

and he said *hey,*
well, I can't cry
and they can't, so you just go ahead

I pushed my face into his chest
to hide its meltedness
and I felt my little breasts push against him
my little stick waist

From then on
first morning thought was always Cousin Groundpigeon
the hump of his back still dreaming away
like a great stirring knot, and up he always
lumbered
fixing a mean fire if there was a fire to be fixed

And did he dream of me? I began to always wonder
and wish it

But no, he didn't dream
of me

I took to making sachets of that sick-sweet herb
that springs up in the hollows where the blisters
runnel, little plastic webbing pouches of smell

I knotted them against my most ripe parts

I took to humming in the day
as we well know my voice is thin but clear
a dark branch
in winter

His hands were broad before and now their rough slow woodenness
inflamed me
the hulking of his shoulders
his few gleaming
teeth

Grandmother always kept me close
in our sleeping line
I think she must have smelled
my wishes

Yes yes
I heard the warning songs
but there are songs
and then
there is the body

I remember, back in the Reddy
there were surges and strikes for years
rolling brownouts and curfews
it was very boring
And then the amperes left and the coast became
impossible

Everyone crinkling away in their plastic bubble hoods
for the inland trek
waddling and drizzling along
in their gizzard tape and wrappings

I couldn't stand that plastic feeling
on my lips, didn't know the melt where the weather touched skin
would take its time

I used to have a lot of things
and I carried them
while everywhere the ground a squeegee as we skimmed along
the old highways, day by day

When the blistering started
I let the things
fall by

Still reach for them

Grandmother reckons we should send our sorrow
right out into the struggle-trees
and the electric puce of the constant dusk
and this one day will help to bring back
the birds

But me
I was always more of one for beaches
never much loved this landscape back
when it was proper

No
I know what I love

On don't-berry nights
I often find myself on all fours
rutting against the gauze of my pleasure cave

A spank of quartz glittering at the edge
of my eye

This time, though, I became a true branch
taut and hard and braced but bendy
and a butcherbird with a blunt beak and a hungry smell
bore down

And then the branch that I was became a nest
I was all tucked into myself and bound to myself
no hands no feet

I heard the church bells of Grandmother's song
clang upside down and down
as the hungry bird
settled and sank himself
inside of me

I came back to myself in a sweat
tangled up in my plastics oh my almanac
where is steady Grou my one
I feel him looking

I see the hump of him across the fire
his eyes are lidded and half in dream he still
is bathing

But
no

The eyes on me are
someone else's

The beak of Cousin Butcher is tearing
and quick and always hungry, but he starts
slipping me roots, choosing his scrounge up close to my knees
my skinny arse

Every time his teeming shadow brushes against me
I look up
to see if Cousin Grou is
watching my way

What's that smell on you?
Butcher whispers one night when Yana
is making the Instrument
buzz

Hot breath he all is
and close

It's called perfume
I say, he says
It's horrible

I would rather smell you

So, as it turns out,
a face
is not essential

As Cousin Grou kept his gaze far and away on the blisters
and this gaze-away grew into a hole
I carried round
I let myself be guided
behind the Resting Trees
I let the one who wanted to
cut away
my smells

I don't know how he got into my cave
don't ask me

You can't be in another's cave
unless you're Gone
as we well know

I felt the licking flamelets of power
as I pushed him off me afterwards
when all he wanted was
another go

Who is it? he would say
Who do you go off to
when you close that eye?

I wonder if
the time he roped me
back
was when he planted
the bad seed

As we well know
it took its root in a halfway place
and now it is
this pain

They sing me all day now
but I am a bent stick
a whimper

Cousin Grou has his woody hand
against my cheek all through the fever
dream

No
not even that
he is off lancing

Oh Grandmother, oh My Almanac, I can be better
I'll give back what I stole
from Yana
I swear

I am not ready for the Trees yet
I never was

COUSIN BUTCHER

I always had a thing for Twig –
Bit of a whinger, mewling in the scrub like a
runt cat –
Nice little body, but.
Figured she'd grown up enough, so I
amped the
campaign
We kept it quiet like, back behind the Trees.
Learned to keep my thumb in her mouth.
The face never worried me:
loved getting it in
from
behind.

So maybe at first it wasn't me she was juicing for –
But I made it me and she liked it.
Saw her moping in Grou's direction
but guess he couldn't get it up for a skinny thief.
And me, I knew where her stash was.

Getting in her cave took time –
Memory's thick
but I still got a bit of before, used to know
how to tip a sucker's trip
full dark,
too easy. Just say, *Mate. Nobody wants you here.*
Whisper it and off he goes, he's gone.

I figured: going full fucken bird
was the way to get a view on all that black,
                                                            find   the
                                                                   slits
There's no magic.
Old crone knows how to make a lab out of
                                                                   fuck   all.
It's a talent.
Why else do you think I stuck around?

Come on, mum, I was *nice*. Told Twig she smelled right.
Told her, see that Gone wrapper up there, that's me next moon
if I don't   get
                                                            a   lick
a little bit of lucky. I'm dying –

And honey kid's gone, sweet scrap
of a weirdo, worming her pictures into our caves
and braiding the camp with her cracked loon play.
        Long gone.

Anyway, after I
                figured the
                                                            breach

I was going good there for a while –
had the bird thing down.
Didn't need to spend every cave night
getting wisty
in here with you, mum.
Had Twig, had our rank little fuck yous
to the *no* songs –
Had Yana being sweet, knotting all dark day and trying for jerkins,
getting fudgy on the Instrument –
Had Steady Groundpigeon with his rock
of a head down, hard out lancing and dragging round
that christ wish –
He can have it.

Me, I could always spot a loner's camp –
sad
scrap
of a picture tacked up on a struggle-tree,
cracked jerry cans and root stash and grot.
Sometimes one of those rabbits with the wrong eyes.
Fully weak
for before
they all are pretty much.
Jesus, mum, I never hurt anyone a knee on the neck
they always wake up from.

Then Twig had to go and get up the spout all sick
and squandered –
Her needs so loud she let herself get picked.

Had Yana and Frogmouth carrying on
at the Instrument Twig in a proper thrash
I couldn't –

Had the old crone telling me: *not the berries*
all: *cave dark wrongly entered*
invites the impotence of a lone roost

Babble. What
would she know, what's she got besides some ash skills,
some fucked vision of all of us dickless and busy like ants.
She shouldn't have tried to stop me.
I needed Twig's blanket for its sprinklemuffin
smell.
So she can mumble bashed over the gone dogs
long as she likes. Stay out my
head

So Twig's in the Trees now, mum.
Butcherbirds, you know? They keep a little larder,
line up their catches for later.

I climbed up and I wedged Twig, she lolled
over the void
like fucken always. Not holding me
back –

I got that thorn in deep. Undid her –
kept the face wrapped & had a taste.
Little earlobe, little strip
of neck.

Over in camp I can hear the hag droning:
the Almanac closes the Almanac closes
And I hear mottled Frogmouth and the pigeon fighting over the salvage
of my name.

Then I sleep, I guess.

And then I can't hear nothing.

COUSIN GROUNDPIGEON

Before, we were all wrapped up tight
in the cloth of ourselves, and all the things
we said and thought cooled in the fridge,
and the fridge ran, and was the things we did,
and made the earth hotter.

I was a teacher in Reddy-by-the-Sea,
half in love with the kids' weird wisdoms
and half wishing to crack open
their little bored-eyed heads.
I lived with a woman I liked,
and tried to desire. Once a year we'd drive
the battered Subaru to a finger of land
and plant grasses and the sprouts of giant flax
as a keep-safe against eroding seas
we didn't quite believe in.

The arguments we used to relish
pitted the proper nouns of countries
and the symbology of their new flags
against each other. Remember countries?
We watched the fire as I watch the fire now,
and the answer is no –

All some system whose distant workings
I squint my mind towards, unlucky.
In the morning we'd toe the fire-bleached
beer cans from the cold coals,
swim in the sea, say sorry,
pick at the plastic tide and fill a plastic bag
with shreddings, or were they dead fish, drive back.
Drive to work. Was always telling myself
I should take the bus, but I liked my calefaction,
my private music, the insulated moment
before the children's loud petitions and tribal pageantry
charged through the linoleum hallways
and used up all the will and patience
sleep had given me back.

I constructed living dioramas
themed around the threatened delicacy of World,
then instructed the children: move the cruel sun
of the heat lamp closer.

I watched their faces crumble,
then I'd get them into a comfort circle.
Next morning, though, they'd be coming in
from the built world, wanting every novelty
it dangled and getting it.

How was I any different?
With my habitats, my entitlements,
my comforts, my holiday waste.

When the winter we're still in started,
curfew shortened the school hours and we all learned
less and less. Surges made all channels of gas and light
too unstable, and the sky got lilac in a way that spooked
even the fix crews, who couldn't dispatch at night,
what with all the lightning striking sideways.

One day, when Humanitarians blocked the freeways
to protest the media muffle on the long-range weather reports,
well, the kids were happy.

Is a society crash like a plane crash?
That sounds awesome
We wouldn't have to come to school!
But I like school
What's a Humanitarian?
Oh I know, it's like a vegetarian, but they eat humans

I saw The End play out in clouds one time
in a private spectacle on a hilltop ruin,
best sky of my life. I spent nearly all
of my before travelling like that.
The cactus powder we whisked set quickly,
a repulsive Jell-O I think of sometimes
when I'm lancing blisters, a stone in the gut
we managed to house long enough
for it to do its work before vomiting the glob
onto the uphill path. We climbed,
and the woman I lived with wouldn't
stop talking and it prickled my brain so I took myself off
just as time began to shimmer from its line
and came peeling free of the cellophane of the moment.

The grass was very grass and down in it I laid.
The wind was racing weather across the astrosphere
and then a jaguar – over the horizon
it reared unmistakably in its cumulus pelt and snarl
and I could have touched it if I'd reached.
It came over me, a menace of intelligent shadow,
and for this reason it is one of the only animal forms
I can still call to memory in this hot perpetual half-light winter.
Behind it trundled a gnashing cavalcade of other beings,
all enormous and World,
and I knew with great certainty that I was privy to a last parade.

All of this was somehow hysterical and wondrous,
and when the medicine had had its show,
it climaxed, and next to me
was sat the devil with the rag eyes, laughing.
His mouth was perfectly spherical as a nought.
I clapped my hands.

How we came to be there and what it was like
to shuffle into the cabin of an aeroplane,
hundreds of people strapped with their private possessions
and wrapped-up foods a fuselage for have,
and on arriving, to ring up persons
continents away and hear leftovers of their voices,
I cannot imagine it anymore.

I did not wonder at it then, and now
when I call a rare warning across the hollow of the scrounge,
I can hear my limit.

It hasn't been easy for me to take on
all Grandmother's words, so I don't.
It's saved us, what she's managed: causing strangers
to make themselves into family.
I see the point of the ritual clustering,
how it helps to speak the same language.
I just can't sing all of its songs.

But I want to be – what? Contributive?
It's a tattered sort of last-gasp help
but strangely less constrained
than the lessons I planned and delivered
while we ate up the world.

Now, when I see devils poling along the dust horizon –
the flapping rags of their eyes,
the bitten bread rolls of their two faces –
I understand them as imprints.

In a world without mirrors, the eye finds a way.

It helps, too, that this one long season is hot,
a haze trapped under the sky's lid.
If this was a true cold winter, think
how we'd be beating our arms against our bodies,
think how we'd be rigid in the sleeping line
against the pricking freeze –

We'd be Gone.

You'd think, then, that we would call this spring, or summer.
But we cannot, and we don't.

In the caves, there's no one person from before
that I visit or summon. Instead, those nights
are like the sex dreams I used to wake up happy from,
guilt torquing the pleasure higher
for how I had not earned it.

My heart these days, it feels edible.
The rest of me: a knot against cessation.

YANA

The cave nights are taking longer and longer to wear off, I am finding. Their visions feather into the day, making my scrounging poor and blurry. My shoulder is a touch horizon I keep trying to look over, and past.

I feel that I have married a sun that never sets.

I don't miss Cousin Twig, exactly, but hers was the hardest Going yet. I can't stop feeling the blank purpose with which we sang her Gone. I try and talk to Butcher, the one we know planted in Twig the painward seed, but his eyes are wild with want and the sorry I feel for him is a putrid taste burden. I face towards her tree, her stiffening wrap, and do a thing like prayer.

We are not supposed to sing her songs but sometimes I catch them in the air and put them in my mouth.

I ask Grandmother what it means to help and she says it is giving a comfort so needed it can't be asked for, and she puts her hands in my hair. When she gave us all a thought of birds to carry in our names, mine was Honeyeater, but I cannot now recall a taste of sweetness. Yana sounds to me more like the nothing sky, the hum of a dry well.

There are rooms I keep finding myself in and in these rooms I put the pen in the unpractised left hand of my child mind, but pens have nothing to spell us anymore, and nor do we have them. I come to, with dust kissing at my eyes. Is it him?

Stroke the blameless dust, says Grandmother.

Grandmother sits heavy-hipped and cross-legged by the almost ringing us and studies the new season, trying to learn the patterns of its skies and thorough dimnesses, and watching for life. Her hands are always busy and if she needs a thing she can't reach, she shouts for it. Lately, she has found a new pigment in the runnels. This is what our hope is made of.

I listen to the others flake the coil of the Instrument at night as I sway my husk.

A fight in camp today. I want to blanch the bruise it left, but in Cousin Butcher, want and sorry have pickled to a whistling rage. This is just the kind of splinter the warnings guard against. Grandmother has been knocked, but somehow it unlatched in her mind a new river of resource. The rest of us argue Butcher's belonging while he fumes off to the Trees.

It is not what he feels that matters. And Twig is Gone, a lost Little Grassbird caged in the purse shape of her own nest.

How can I learn to belong here? I ask Grandmother and she says, You have to know what heat is. Go into the heat until your edges rasp and mouth the graph of it. I imagine making newly such a sound on the cell rust of the Instrument might help, and also talk. But back in the Reddy, my deepest life only needed two people and now those two people are Gone.

What does it mean to love? I ask Grandmother. She says, It is taking the self out of the self, and smudging the gold from the morning.

Here we have lilac and grey-green and red dust and rivulets. We have white and black. But no gold, and no morning.

YAWNING MOON

All the gone ones now bring me their songs,
rhythm their electrical flicker.
As in life, they are both here and gone,
a lack and an asking.

Poor things, they lay
their non-bodies down against my face,
and become new shadows.
Song finds song, until all there is
is a hum
that falls and rises.

Down there, the human dusk, I can see
is baked in.

Mirrors have lost their hold and use,
as has what I hear them calling love –
a curious and unpredictable energy.
I can't pretend to understand it.

Stuck seeds are not the only reason for their warnings.
Grandmothers, I see, are the ones
folding the desert up into a blanket,
checking its fabric for burn holes.

Poor things. So feeling all the time,
and needy with it, not like the animals –
I once so enjoyed
the limitations of their simple violence.

Yes. So unlike the animals.
I watched the noisiest of them
misbelieve the sea
and devils formed at every reflection
as they cut themselves apart.

There have always come collapsings,
and there was never any sense to talk of fault.
But I admit, I am impressed
at this one's roaring swiftness.

YANA

Grandmother says a child is a lovely and perilous thing for which to be scrounging. We did bring a child to the green-desert, but she went: not to the Resting Trees because children don't have a song –

they are the singing.

She kept herself close to the karst of the Almanac, and drawings she made with a pigment paste on the roof of its mouth we kept as Story. Grandmother says Story is a high and nourishing thing for which to be scrounging. Story completes us. But what is completion? Permission to draw a circle around something?

The child's brother had had a natural talent for locks and fastenings, but then the lightning. The child's sister had needed the gaze of everyone as a species of shelter, but then the rain. We kept the child umbrellaed in swaddling the whole trek long and the drizzle couldn't pock her jubilance. Her cheeks kept their texture of boiled egg.

Oh, egg.

Even in retreat, hiding was a game. Carrying was a game. Who would carry her animal? Who would carry the vehicle of her dreaming body? She drew a kind of language made of circles and the bowls that bodies make when they are sat in a posture of care. She drew the cousins until their outlines blurred and they became a murmuration.

She drew a watch of night-birds in perpetual motion. It astounded us. She was only a child.

Some of the things she drew were true and difficult to bear. A woman shopping. A letter sealed and sleeping. A wave made wholly of human hands. A fire-shouting aeroplane.

She would not paint herself or any face and refused a new name from Grandmother. We called her child, the child, or honey. If I asked questions at that time, Grandmother would point with her mouth to where the child was mucking in the river hollow or clambering Cousin Frogmouth's back to gain a view of all that we had left. When the child would dance to usher in the cave nights, Grandmother wanted us to see the dance's function. Child as cipher. Cambering. She hardly seemed able to think of herself.

But her green eyes rapid like water. The fact of her beauty. Thin though she was, even her grey pallor shone like silver.

We watched her and watched her and what we felt was love.

One day, sitting with the Instrument and watching the child make Story, she tired and I took her in my arms and she asked me to tell her something. What shall I tell you honey? Her head was warm and I liked this being needed. Tell me why we had the Radius, she said, and why we have the rashing. Tell me like you're telling Grandmother's grandmother's grandmother.

Shhh, I said, and murmured *sing, choirs of angels*. Nothing will ever happen, I told her, and in that moment I felt a certainty that I could make it so.

After the child got rashed and some of us went wild with cure-thinking, Grandmother got fierce. She used my name of Honeyeater. Said love is a dangerous and childlike thing for which to be scrounging.

Wildness will not keep us alive, she said, and we must draw a circle around it. The watch must stay in flock and keep moving.

She took the child away for days and days, and when she returned she was alone. A loose thread in me cauterised the chasm shut.

I have since tried to confine that feeling to the cave.

Today we are moving again up the river hollow because the roots here are exhausted. We wear the blankets and carry Almanac's arcana in our heads, as we will have to remake them. As we walk, I finger the buoyant skull of a bird, sometimes holding it up to the sky. A practice in glimpsing.

At every new camp, the flight of ourselves is smaller and smaller. I can barely remember Cousin Twig's song, though I recall when Grandmother hollered for a tool or a beaker she would pretend to be deaf as a microwave. All of us could feel as well that seep of Butcher's restless rage. I feel it sometimes now – This – cracked possibilities

agitating towards a breach –

But she 'knows I'm gonna stay'.

I say to myself, *Yana – stop that thought – listen to Grandmother.*

At the new camp, mottled Frogmouth finds a wheel well fine for trying fires in and a torn set of car doors oxidised by air and prior enamels. We drag and lean them for a windbreak, they will do.

COUSIN FROGMOUTH

Before he died my Dmitri said to me –
I will come and get you when it's time to go

He hasn't come for me yet – *Don't be afraid*
he said – *No one gets to live twice*

After the shocks stopped rolling in you saw folk everywhere
go strange – They'd seen the void and it dazzled them blind

It isn't panic that takes hold of people – It's that they can't
get unmoored from the old story – It swallows their tongues

But next door my old neighbour with her bush eyes –
She'd been drilling at the End at every season

We'd hear her in the orchard doing her proclamations
and painting the trees white

Asking us round to get a circle going – Salt and branches –
Waiting up for the world to end – Is it any madder than the rest?

She knew every sprout and bush and tree and every night-mammal
She had her Last Manifest and her Log of the Gone

Dmitri and me we had a cellar, petrol, a well – We had a gun –
We had the dogs Whiskey and Mum

Used to be I could make a dead truck purr
I could whittle wood to lace

Now it's a wood age stone age blister age –
Time has bitten its own tail

When the looters came Dmitri stood at our door
with the rifle wagging

Right where I'd carved two old moons
with their bellies in crossover – We had a life so

Man pulls the trigger but God carries the bullet
my Dmitri used to say

It happened slow – I saw his head sink down to his chest –
Just like a sunflower – Two petals one petal

The earth will take anyone when it's their time
Or the Trees will –

Leaving the farm it felt like hell – A screw turned backwards
Til you strip its thread

Whiskey and Mum with their bellies low to fizzing ground
Like all was off – And it was

'In a little while from now – If I'm not feeling any less sour
I promise myself to treat myself and visit a nearby tower' –

We all have a song – We all have a cave
where the shape of our best gone touch keeps on whistling

The old woman goes on about *building no love towers* –
But I see the shine she carries for Yana

As my Dmitri used to say – *In the bladesmith's house*
All the knives are made of wood

Night time the pains come twisting up my leg –
All my nerves are scorched fire and gravy

When my old neighbour goes Forgetting I wrap up
Take a day to try out death in the Trees –

But hunger heats the wanting to lay down the needing to get up
It all takes a mind off perfect misery –

And a little joy did sail back in when I got
salved – There's nowhere else I'm needed

Even a bird has to love its nest – Even a moment is enough

When my leg was well again I looked at our diminishment
Thought about going back for Butcher

But the boy had looting in his face
Plain as an eye colour

I recalled his taunt when we got our names –
Sit an owl on a post he said

And walk round it in a circle –
It'll watch you til it wrings its own neck

A boy like that can't understand
Now we all have to backwards

The pleasure of the caves of course
has always helped with the keep-on –

But now the old woman who once lived next door says
we need to give it up for different work

Seven generations back – That's the number of kin
we need to tell this Story

What we made – The Radius the blistered hills
the struggle-trees – The struckdown

There's no rapture in witness
I would rather be with my Dmitri

And you know people – There's always some distraction
Even when they're Gone

My Dmitri has a story – A man saw Christ
led past his window – Bowed as a shoehorn

Saw Him stumble and cry out – The man almost got up
and went out to witness – But he had a toothache –

That's how it is – People aren't going to listen –
But here's what we do, says the old woman

We just keep telling them

COUSIN BUTCHER

days   fucken days
            days

don't-berries   split   my   mouth some naught

                                                                    I –

Twig's   gone   nasty
                                            black   little   fingerpads
            I jerky

                                                        Mum, you there?

      black   little   thumb

heat
                        and   nothing   keep on

or don't
                                            hey honeykid
                                                              we're done out here
            send   a new picture

YAWNING MOON

Those still here, like me, pace and watch
in the residue of double death
while the prize bloodstone of carbon's wild possibilities
leaches of its colour.

We did   *we did*
that sad few sing now
every time I yawn because the long night's coming –

We did   *what we did*   *what we did*
they sing their story of the coming-about –
fires, surges, blisters,
the blip of their built world eating up all the green and other.
Some hard song it is, deafness and ravening.

How little they know.
Never have I watched an animal become so severed from the hum
but I see them humming now,
rocking themselves outside of time and hunger
and calling all the new shadows to witness,
as if life depended.

It's another day over, beautiful and bad.
Life does depend
but the Gone ones are far asleep
and I myself am very tired, though I do feel them
stirring a little in their shadow-nests,
trying to answer to the call.

ACKNOWLEDGEMENTS

I want to thank A Few Don'ts and Desperate Literature for drafting and moral support, and The Longwood Appreciation Society and Cumulus for space to write. Thanks to Amy Brown, Terry Craven, Rose Currie, David Harsent, Shari Kocher, Bella Li and Erin Scudder for their insight and advice, and Kent MacCarter for his piercing editorial guidance. Thank always, to my family, and above all, to Dom Czapla, my reason and my best taboo.

Part of this book was written on Taungurung, Bunurong and Wurundjeri country, where I live as a guest. If we can listen to First Nations people, we might stand a chance.

Joan Fleming's honours include the Biggs Poetry Prize, a Creative New Zealand writing fellowship, and the Harri Jones Memorial Prize from the Hunter Writers Centre. She holds a PhD in ethnopoetics from Monash University, work that has been shortlisted for the Helen Anne Bell Poetry Prize. Her literary citizenship includes serving on the programming team for the Unamuno Author Series in Madrid and is the Aotearoa/New Zealand Commissioning Editor for *Cordite Poetry Review*.